QIN SHI HUANGDI

First Emperor of China

Peggy Pancella

Heinemann Library
Chicago, Illinois

Customer Service 888-454-2279
Visit our website at www.heinemannlibrary.com

Designed by Lisa Buckley
Maps by John Fleck
Photo research by Julie Laffin
Printed and Bound in the United States by Lake Book Manufacturing, Inc.

08 07 06 05 04
10 9 8 7 6 5 4 3 2 1

Library of Congress Cataloging-in-Publication Data
Pancella, Peggy.
   Qin Shi Huangdi / Peggy Pancella.
      p. cm. -- (Historical biographies)
Audience: "Age: 7-9."
Summary: Presents an overview of Qin Shi Huangdi's life as well as his influence on history and the world.
Includes bibliographical references and index.
   ISBN 1-4034-3704-1 (Library Binding-hardcover) -- ISBN 1-4034-3712-2 (Paperback)
   1. 880-06 Qin Shihuang, Emperor of China, 259-210 B.C.--Juvenile literature. 2. China--Kings and rulers--Biography--Juvenile literature. 3. China--History--Qin dynasty, 221-207 B.C.--Juvenile literature. [1. Qin Shihuang, Emperor of China, 259-210 B.C. 2. Kings, queens, rulers, etc. 3. China--History--Qin dynasty, 221-207 B.C.] I. Title. II. Series.
   DS747.9.Q254P36 2003
   931'.04--dc21
                              2003005922

Acknowledgments
The author and publisher are grateful to the following for permission to reproduce copyright material: Icon, p. 26 Giraudon/Art Resource; pp. 4, 14, 16, 17 The Granger Collection; pp. 7, 18, 19, 22, 24 Ancient Art & Architecture Collection LTD; p. 8 The Art Archive; p. 9 Royal Ontario Museum/Corbis; pp. 10, 11, 12 Cultural Relics Publishing House; p. 13 Erich Lessing/Art Resource, NY; p. 15 The British Museum; p. 20 Dallas and John Heaton/Corbis; p. 21 The Nelson-Atkins Museum of Art, Kansas City, Missouri; p. 23 Art Resource, NY; p. 25 Asian Art & Archaeology, Inc./Corbis; p. 27 Keren Su/Corbis; p. 28 Bruce Coleman Inc.; p. 29 Ashmolean Museum Oxford.

Cover photograph: The Granger Collection, (background) Réunion des Musées Nationaux/Art Resource, NY

Special thanks to Michelle Rimsa for her comments in the preparation of this book.

Some words are shown in bold, **like this.** You can find out what they mean by looking in the glossary.

Many Chinese names and terms may be found in the pronunciation guide.

For more information on the image of Qin Shi Huangdi that appears on the cover of this book, turn to page 4.

Contents

Who Was Qin Shi Huangdi? 4

A Child of Qin 6

Daily Life 8

Earlier Rulers 10

Rising to Power 12

The New Emperor 14

Belief Systems 16

New Methods for a New Empire 18

Building Projects 20

Destroying Thought 22

The Fear of Death 24

A Final Tour 26

After Qin Shi Huangdi 28

Glossary 30

Time Line 31

Pronunciation Guide 31

More Books to Read 31

Index 32

Who Was Qin Shi Huangdi?

Qin Shi Huangdi lived long ago in what is now China. At first, he ruled only a small part of the land. Later, he united many kingdoms and ruled as **emperor**. Shi Huangdi made rules that helped make his country run better.

The world in Qin Shi Huangdi's time

At the time Shi Huangdi lived, people in many parts of the world struggled for power. Some countries, such as Greece, took over other lands. The defeated lands and people became part of an **empire**.

Shi Huangdi lived in eastern Asia. At the time, this area did not have the same countries we know today. Instead, there were many populations of people living in small areas. The people in these areas did not get along. Each ruler hoped to build an empire by taking over the other areas.

How do we know about Qin Shi Huangdi?

Most of what we know about Shi Huangdi comes from the *Shiji*, a book by a man named Sima Qian. However, no one knows how much of the *Shiji* is true. Sima Qian never knew Shi Huangdi, and he wrote the book more than 100 years after the emperor's death.

▶ **This is a painting of Qin Shi Huangdi. Qin is his family name, or last name, even though it comes first. When he was a boy, he was known by the name Zheng.**

Historians also studied other information to learn about Shi Huangdi. A few other writings and various artwork show more about people and events of the time. In addition, **archaeologists** have found **artifacts**, including bones and weapons. They also looked at the **ruins** of old buildings. Comparing all this information gave a clearer picture of Shi Huangdi's life.

▼ This map shows the area in Asia that Shi Huangdi ruled and where the country of China is located today.

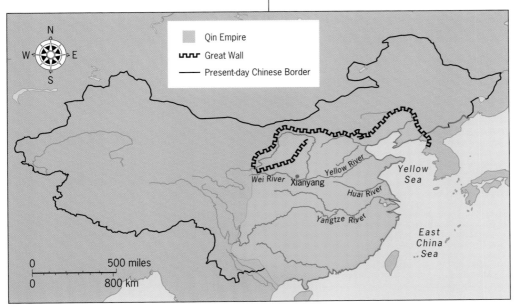

Key dates

259 B.C.E.	Birth of Zheng (later named Qin Shi Huangdi)
246 B.C.E.	Zheng becomes king of Qin
238 B.C.E.	Zheng rules Qin alone
221 B.C.E.	Zheng unites China as Qin Shi Huangdi
210 B.C.E.	Death of Qin Shi Huangdi

Watch the dates

The letters B.C.E. after a year date means "before the common era." This is used instead of the older abbreviation B.C. The years are counted backwards toward zero. Historians are not sure about some dates of Qin Shi Huangdi's life. You may see different dates in different books.

A Child of Qin

Shi Huangdi was born in about 259 B.C.E. His mother was named Zhao Ji, and his father was King Zhuang Xiang of Qin. At birth, Shi Huangdi was given the name Zheng.

The Warring States

Very little is known about Zheng's early life. He was born during a time called the Warring States Period. The land we now call China was divided into many separate small kingdoms, known as states. Each kingdom had its own rulers and own ways of doing things.

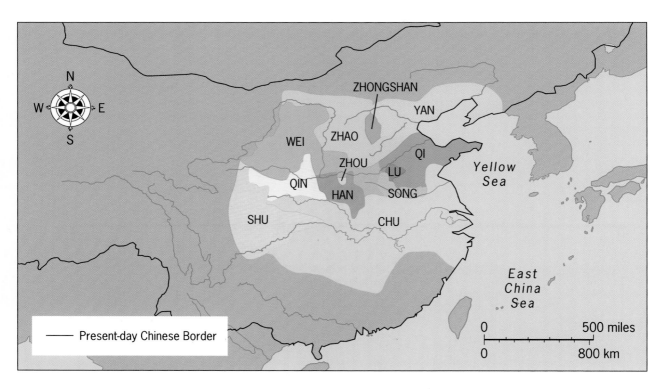

▲ This map shows the original Warring States. They began as small kingdoms. Little by little, some of the larger kingdoms took over the smaller ones. By the time Zheng came to power, there were only seven main kingdoms left. These were known as the Seven States.

These kingdoms had been fighting for hundreds of years. Each state wanted to be more powerful than the others. One way to get power was to control more land. When the states fought, the winner would take over the loser's lands. Winners also controlled the people in those lands.

The kingdom of Qin

Zheng was born in Qin, one of the largest and strongest of the Warring States. It was located in the western part of the area. The people of Qin were strong fighters. They made many powerful attacks on enemy kingdoms. They also fought to protect their own lands when others attacked.

Zheng's father, Zhuang Xiang, was the king of Qin. As ruler, he controlled Qin's army and made rules for his people to follow. When Qin took over other lands, Zhuang Xiang ruled them, too. Some of the people did not want him to be in charge, and they did not obey very well. The king had to be a strong leader to keep order among so many people from different places.

▼ These are spears that were used as weapons by soldiers in the Warring States.

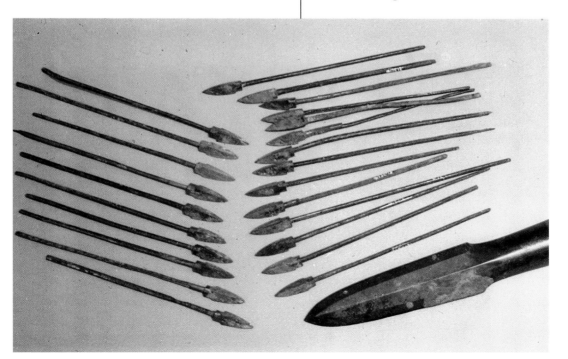

Daily Life

Although Zheng lived in a time of war, his childhood did not involve fighting. We do not know much about his early life, but it was probably similar to the lives of other **noble** families of the time.

Life in a noble family

In Zheng's time, people belonged to four social groups. The most important people were nobles and **scholars.** Zheng's family was part of this group. Second came farmers, who produced food for everyone. Artists and craftspeople came next, and merchants and traders were least important, although they were usually rich.

▼ **This modern painting shows what a market in ancient China might have looked like.**

Most nobles were rich and powerful, with servants to do work for them. Some people were born into noble families. Others became nobles by doing well in war or by working as government leaders. Sometimes, nobles had to work or visit the **emperor's** court, but mostly they enjoyed life at home. Their houses were often as fancy as small palaces, with courtyards and gardens.

Nobles wore fine **silk** clothes and beautiful jewelry. Some nobles' children had **tutors** or went to school, but many got little or no education.

▲ This statue shows two men playing *liubo. Liubo* was a game like chess that was played by people in ancient China.

Life in the city and country

Many people lived in cities and towns. Here, houses were smaller and closer together. People had many kinds of jobs. Some bought and sold items at the city's market. Others did jobs for people, like cutting hair or fixing carts. The people wore simple clothes made of plain cloth.

The largest number of people were poor farmers. Like city workers, they wore simple clothing and lived in small, plain houses. Farmers worked hard all year long, planting and tending their crops. Children also learned how to do farmwork, and they often did not go to school.

Games and entertainment

Life in Zheng's time was not all about work. People enjoyed many kinds of entertainment, including dancing, juggling, music, and storytelling. They played card games and board games similar to chess. There were **festivals** throughout the year, too. The most important one was the New Year festival. People celebrated with parades, feasts, kite flying, and fireworks.

Earlier Rulers

Prince Zheng knew he would rule Qin someday. To learn how to rule well, Zheng studied the lives of earlier rulers—especially his father and grandfather.

Stories from the past

Zheng's grandfather, Duke Xiao, had ruled in about 350 B.C.E. A duke was the highest level of **noble**, with the power of a king. To make the kingdom stronger, Duke Xiao created strict new laws and punishments. The people were afraid to break the laws. So, they did what they were told, and the kingdom ran smoothly.

Duke Xiao was to be replaced when he died by either Ankuo or Xiao's relative Zizhu. Ankuo was the oldest son, or **crown prince**, so he was expected to rule after the duke died. Zizhu was not expected to rule. As a result, the duke used him to make a peace agreement with the nearby state of Zhao. He sent Zizhu to Zhao as a **hostage**—a sign of his promise not to attack Zhao. The people of Zhao knew that Xiao would not attack because he would not want to harm his own son.

◄ Shang Yang, shown at left, was one of Duke Xiao's closest advisers. He pushed the duke to show his power by treating his people strictly.

In Zhao, Zizhu met a merchant named Lu Buwei. Lu Buwei had a plan. He wanted Zizhu to become king instead of Ankuo. Lu Buwei hoped Zizhu would make him his **adviser**. Lu Buwei knew that one of Ankuo's wives had no children. She was very sad. She wanted a son to continue the royal family. Lu Buwei suggested that she adopt Zizhu. The young man would bring her much honor when he became ruler. Ankuo's wife quickly agreed.

The new king

Duke Xiao died in 251 B.C.E., and Ankuo became ruler. But Ankuo ruled for only one year before he died. Zizhu became king. He took the royal name Zhuang Xiang and rewarded Lu Buwei by making him a close adviser. Lu Buwei also received a large sum of money.

▲ Lu Buwei, above, used his friendship with Zhuang Xiang to become rich and powerful.

Zheng's parents

Historians know that King Zhuang Xiang's wife Zhao Ji was Zheng's mother. But they are not sure who Zheng's father was. Both Zhuang Xiang and his adviser Lu Buwei loved Zhao Ji. No one knows for certain which man was Zheng's father. But Zhuang Xiang raised Zheng as his own son.

Rising to Power

King Zhuang Xiang ruled Qin for only a few years. He died in 247 B.C.E., and his son Zheng became king soon after. He was just thirteen years old.

Early years of Zheng's rule

Because King Zheng was so young, his mother and Lu Buwei ruled for him at first. Lu Buwei knew how to run the government, and he was also a smart businessperson. While he ruled for Zheng, Lu Buwei used his power to make laws that helped him get very rich.

In 238 B.C.E., King Zheng was finally old enough to take over. Around the same time, his mother and Lu Buwei were caught in a **scandal** at the palace. Lu Buwei was sent away, and Zheng began to rule at last.

A strong leader

Not much is known about King Zheng's personal life. Like most kings of his time, he had several wives. He also had more than twenty children, but we do not know their names or anything about them. **Historians** do know that Zheng was a strong leader who was not afraid to make changes. He planned his actions carefully so that he could gain more power. He worked hard, often late into the night.

▶ **This drawing shows Li Si, King Zheng's trusted adviser.**

With the help of a trusted **adviser** named Li Si, Zheng began to organize the kingdom. Zheng gave people certain jobs, mostly as farmers or soldiers. He trained the army to make his troops strong. Little by little, Zheng's army attacked the other Warring States. Han was first to fall, in 230 B.C.E. Next came Zhao, Wei, Chu, and Yan. Only Qi was left, and it was conquered in 221 B.C.E. Now, Zheng controlled all of the land that would one day become China.

▶ **This statue was found near Qin Shi Huangdi's tomb. It may have been made to look like an actual soldier in the king's army.**

Trying to kill the king

Zheng was a strong leader, but not everyone liked his ideas. A man named Jing Ke thought that killing Zheng might end the **empire's** power. He wrapped a poisoned **dagger** in a map and went to the palace. He offered the map to King Zheng, but quickly pulled out the dagger and tried to stab the king. Zheng ran, and his guards caught and killed Jing Ke.

The New Emperor

King Zheng now ruled all the Warring States. To show his power, Zheng gave himself a more important title— Shi Huangdi, the "First **August Emperor.**" His full name, including his family name, was now Qin Shi Huangdi. All his lands now shared the name Qin (sometimes written "Ch'in"). This is where we get the name China.

A new order

One of Shi Huangdi's first projects as emperor was to organize the different lands he ruled. In his capital city, Xianyang, he built copies of palaces from the defeated states. He forced rich and powerful families from each of the Warring States to move into palaces. There, his leaders could control these families more easily.

Shi Huangdi also made people from the other states give up their weapons. His men collected weapons from all over the **empire.** In Xianyang, the weapons were melted down.

▲ No one knows what Qin Shi Huangdi really looked like. Many images of him, such as this Chinese drawing, show a large, bearded man.

▲ This is a small tiger statue called a tally. Shi Huangdi used tallies to make sure his orders were carried out correctly.

Changes in government

Shi Huangdi changed the way the government was set up. He divided the land into 36 sections and sent three of his own men to lead each section. Before, only certain powerful people could hold important jobs like these. Fathers passed their jobs on to their sons when they died. But now, Shi Huangdi tried to choose talented people who he thought would do well.

Shi Huangdi kept control by making detailed rules for these workers. They got rewards when they did well, but were severely punished or fired when they were lazy or failed to do their job. Shi Huangdi probably thought that setting up the government while keeping overall control for himself was some of his most important work.

Tiger tallies

All of the Warring States' soldiers were joined into one giant army. However, Shi Huangdi wanted to be sure that only he could give his **generals** orders. So, he gave each general half of a little tiger statue called a tally. A messenger who delivered orders carried the other half of the tally to give to the general. If the two halves matched up, the general could be sure that the orders really had come from the emperor.

Belief Systems

When Shi Huangdi came to power, his people followed several different religions. He combined parts of each faith in deciding how to rule the **empire**.

Confucianism and Taoism

One important set of Chinese beliefs was Confucianism, taught by a **scholar** named Confucius (551–479 B.C.E.). He believed that people should love and obey their parents and other adults. They should be happy with who they were and be kind, fair, and honest toward others. Confucius taught that rulers should be brave and wise. They should keep peace by treating all their people well.

Another belief system, Taoism, was taught by Lao Zi, who was born in about 604 B.C.E. The Tao, or "Way," meant that people should live in **harmony** with nature. Followers of the Tao would be happy and live long lives. Taoism also taught that leaders should not force people to follow too many rules.

◄ Many people in ancient China followed the teachings of Confucius. This image of Confucius was found in the Chinese city of Xian.

Qin Shi Huangdi and Legalism

For people who were used to war, these ideas about kindness and peace probably seemed strange. However, Shi Huangdi liked the idea that people should respect their **ancestors** and rulers. He was interested in a well-run society, and he wanted to live in harmony with nature. But he did not agree that rulers should be kind and gentle. He thought strong laws were important to control the country.

▲ Lao Zi's name means "Old Master." His teachings are still followed in China. He is shown above in a painting from the 1200s.

Both Shi Huangdi and his **adviser** Li Si became followers of another system called Legalism. Confucianism and Taoism taught that people were basically good and should be treated well. But Legalism taught that people should be forced to obey. Rulers should be all-powerful and did not have to take advice from anyone. Legalism included strict laws with harsh punishments for people who disobeyed.

Yin and yang

Many ancient Chinese beliefs focused on order and harmony. People thought that things in the world needed to stay in balance. This *taiji* symbol shows two equal and opposite forces (yin and yang) that balance each other. The yin can mean dark, cool, woman, and quiet. The yang can stand for light, heat, man, and noise. The Chinese believed that the world needed equal amounts of these things.

New Methods for a New Empire

Each Warring State had done things its own way. Now Shi Huangdi wanted them all to do things in the same ways. He thought this would make life easier and run more smoothly.

Making things work together

First, Shi Huangdi chose a type of money for everyone to use. Buying and selling were easier with only one kind of money. The money came in coins that had holes so the coins could be tied on a string.

Shi Huangdi also designed items in standard sizes and weights. Now, people could agree on how large or heavy things were. People buying certain amounts of products could be sure they got what they paid for.

One unusual change was that all carts' wheels had to be the same distance apart. China's roads were rough, and cart wheels made ruts, or tracks, in the ground. Carts with evenly spaced wheels could travel in the same ruts. This was easier than each cart making its own path. Shi Huangdi also had more roads built to make travel easier.

▲ Shi Huangdi's new coins were easy to use and carry around. This coin is from about 220 B.C.E.

18

Communicating across the country

An important change was Shi Huangdi's creation of one system of writing. People could communicate more easily—but not everyone wanted to change. **Scholars** had to copy books into the new writing so people could still read them. The new **script** reduced the number of characters, or signs, to about 3,000. It also made the characters simpler.

Shi Huangdi wanted to see how his ideas were working. He made several trips to various parts of the **empire**. He put up some pillars, or tall posts, in certain parts. Writing on the pillars told about the great things he was doing.

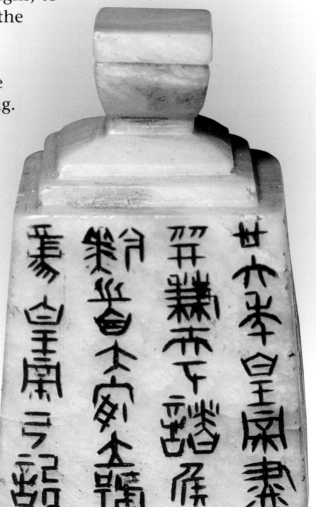

▶ A measuring weight from Shi Huangdi's time is shown here. Shi Huangdi introduced a standard system of measurement to China.

Chinese script
Unlike the letters of the alphabets used to write many other languages, Chinese characters are pictographs. This means they are small drawings of things. Examples of Chinese script can be seen on the weight above.

Building Projects

Shi Huangdi wanted to protect himself and his land from outsiders. He also wanted to show his power. To do this, he started several important building projects.

The Great Wall of China

Different kingdoms in China always built walls for protection. Shi Huangdi wanted to join these short walls into one large wall. It would mark the edge of the **empire** and guard against attacks. He chose a **general**, Meng Tian, to oversee the builders.

Meng Tian took about 300,000 workers to northern China. Many prisoners were also forced to help as part of their punishment. The wall took ten years to build. The Chinese call it "the wall of 10,000 *li*." A *li* is a Chinese measurement of distance—10,000 *li* would be about 1,900 to 2,600 miles (3,000 to 4,100 kilometers) long.

▲ The Great Wall of China is also called the "Wall of Tears." Many workers died while building it. Some are even buried inside.

Palaces and tombs

In Xianyang, Shi Huangdi built a palace called the Afang palace for himself. It was much larger than other palaces of the time. It could hold thousands of people in its large halls. Covered roadways and passages connected the Afang palace to 270 other palaces and **pavilions**.

One passage led to Shi Huangdi's **tomb** at Mount Li. Workers had begun building there as early as 246 B.C.E., when Zheng had first come to power. More than 700,000 men helped with the project. However, they still did not finish it before Shi Huangdi died 36 years later! The tomb contained amazing treasures. Hidden pits nearby were filled with thousands of life-sized statues, probably meant to protect Shi Huangdi after he died.

▲ This model of an ancient Chinese house was found in a tomb. Treasures like this model were also found in Shi Huangdi's tomb.

Feng shui

When Shi Huangdi designed buildings, he probably followed the rules of *feng shui*. This system is a way of organizing the natural environment. It tells where to place furniture, plants, mirrors, and other objects so everything will be in balance. People thought that arranging buildings using *feng shui* would make the owners healthy, rich, and powerful. Many people still use *feng shui* today.

Destroying Thought

Shi Huangdi made all his people use the same kinds of money, writing, and measurements. He also wanted people to think the same way about things, but people did not like being told what to think.

Burning the books

Shi Huangdi thought that his changes made life better. However, many people did not like his ideas. Li Si heard the people saying bad things about the **emperor**. He suggested a way to stop the people's grumbling.

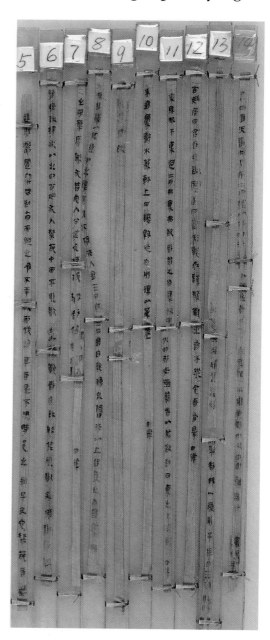

Li Si said that almost all books should be burned. Then no one could read the ideas they contained. People could learn only what the government told them. Shi Huangdi agreed to this plan. In 213 B.C.E., he ordered **scholars** to turn in all their books. Only books about subjects like medicine, farming, and the history of Qin could be saved. Anyone who did not go along with this decision could be punished or killed.

▶ **Many books in Shi Huangdi's time were made from thin strips of wood tied together.**

Killing the scholars

The book burnings shocked many people. They did not know what to do. Shi Huangdi heard that the people—even his own scholars—were complaining. This made him very angry.

Shi Huangdi realized that these people no longer supported him. He wanted them to stop complaining. In 212 B.C.E., he sent some scholars to help build the Great Wall. Conditions there were unpleasant, and the work was hard. He also picked 460 of the scholars and had them buried alive.

▲ This artwork shows Shi Huangdi burning books and killing scholars at the same time. One scholar is begging for the emperor, shown seated at the top, to spare his life.

Shi Huangdi thought that by doing these things, the scholars would not bother him anymore.

Qin Shi Huangdi's weakening power

Book burning and killing scholars were both cruel moves. Yet these actions did not end the people's complaints. Instead, more and more people spoke out against Shi Huangdi. They did not respect his leadership as much as they had before. In fact, some of them thought he might be going crazy! Shi Huangdi's actions created many new enemies.

The Fear of Death

In many ways, Qin Shi Huangdi was a strong leader. He tried to set up his **empire** so that it ran smoothly and to protect it from enemies. However, he also had a secret weakness—he was afraid of dying.

Living in fear

As **emperor**, Shi Huangdi was famous and important. Many people praised him, but others did not like him. They thought he was too cruel and made too many changes. Some people just complained about the emperor. At least three people actually tried to kill him.

The attacks on his life made Shi Huangdi very fearful. He began hiding in his palaces and sleeping in a different place each night. Only a few people were allowed to know where he was, and anyone who told would be killed.

Magic and signs

While Shi Huangdi was trying to stay safe, he was also looking for a way to live forever. He invited magicians to his court to see if they could make a special **potion** for him.

▼ Shi Huangdi and his traveling partners took two covered carriages like the one below. No one knew which carriage Shi Huangdi was in.

He also traveled through China's countryside. He was looking for a mysterious land that might have the secret to endless life.

Like many people of his time, Shi Huangdi believed in omens, or signs of what was going to happen. Events such as floods, earthquakes, and comets all had meanings—some good and some bad. Toward the end of his reign, Shi Huangdi believed he received many frightening messages through signs like these. He was certain that his life was in danger.

▼ It took hundreds of jade pieces to build an ancient Chinese burial suit like this one.

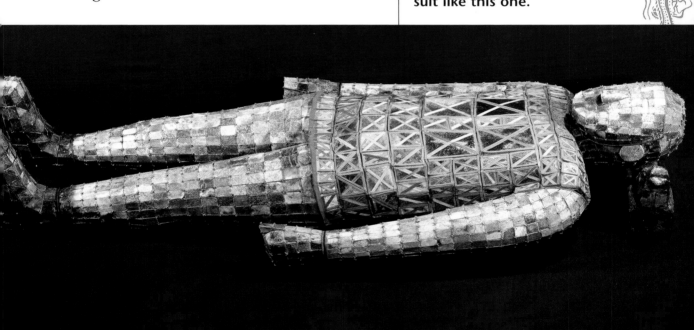

Jade

The ancient Chinese prized jade, a green mineral, even more than gold or silver. Jade was used to make jewelry, statues, and other items. People wore jade pieces or ate powdered jade because they believed it would make them live longer. Some important people were buried in suits made of jade. They thought it would protect their bodies from decay. **Historians** do not know if Shi Huangdi was buried in jade, because his body has not been found.

A Final Tour

Late in 211 B.C.E., Shi Huangdi made one last search for the secret to living forever. He took Li Si, his favorite son Hu Hai, and a group of others with him.

Growing troubles

The journey was difficult for Shi Huangdi. He worked so hard that he grew tired and weak. He may also have been accidentally poisoning himself. He liked to test his magicians' **potions**, but some of these included dangerous substances such as **mercury** and **phosphorus.** No one realized then that eating these substances can kill you.

The group finally headed back to Xianyang, but Shi Huangdi grew weaker and weaker. In the summer of 210 B.C.E., he wrote to his oldest son, Fu Su. He wanted Fu Su to take over as **emperor** after his death. Qin Shi Huangdi asked Hu Hai's **tutor**, Zhao Gao, to deliver the letter. Soon afterward he died. He was only about 49 years old.

◀ Qin Shi Huangdi, shown here being carried, never made it home from his last journey through his **empire.**

Choosing a different ruler

Zhao Gao never went to Fu Su. He wanted Hu Hai to become emperor instead. So he and Li Si wrote a fake letter to Fu Su. Their letter scolded Fu Su for behaving badly. It told him to kill himself as punishment. Fu Su was used to doing what his father told him, so he took his own life with a sword. Now, Hu Hai could become the next emperor.

Li Si and the others did not want anyone to know that Shi Huangdi was dead. They hid his body in one of his covered carriages. However, the summer heat soon made the dead body start to stink. Li Si brought along a cart of smelly fish to cover the smell of the dead body.

▶ **Shi Huangdi might have hoped these statues would keep him safe after he died.**

The terra cotta army

Archaeologists have discovered several pits in the ground near Qin Shi Huangdi's **tomb.** Each pit contains painted statues made of a dried clay called **terra cotta.** The statues of soldiers, horses, and carts are lined up like an army ready to go to war. Many of the soldiers carry weapons. Some **historians** think that the statues were modeled after real people.

After Qin Shi Huangdi

Qin Shi Huangdi's group headed for Xianyang. When they arrived, it was announced that Shi Huangdi had died. Hu Hai claimed power for himself, taking the name Er Shi, which meant the "Second **Emperor**."

The downfall of Qin

Er Shi was only twenty years old, so he trusted his **advisers** to help him. However, they did not always do what was best. Zhao Gao was especially greedy. He told Hu Hai to get rid of anyone who might compete for power, including family members and Li Si.

Er Shi was not very interested in ruling, so he agreed to let Zhao Gao run things. Zhao Gao raised taxes and made stronger punishments for breaking laws. Many people fought against these changes. In 207 B.C.E., Hu Hai killed himself when he thought the palace was under attack. Soon after, the **empire** split into small kingdoms again, and it was several years before a strong new leader came to power.

▼ **This photo shows a marker near Shi Huangdi's tomb.**

That leader, Liu Bang, began the Han **dynasty**, one of the most famous and important in Chinese history.

Remembering Qin Shi Huangdi

When Qin Shi Huangdi ruled, many of his decisions seemed harsh and unfair. People obeyed mainly because they feared for their lives. Some **historians** think he tried to make too many changes too quickly.

However, many of the emperor's changes were lasting ones. Later rulers copied the kinds of laws, government, and army Shi Huangdi used. His systems of writing, money, and measurement have also survived with only a few changes. The Great Wall of China successfully protected the empire, and much of it still stands. Even the book burnings had a positive result. Later, people learned how important written history was.

Qin Shi Huangdi was a strong leader who was sometimes cruel. He united China under one ruler for the first time. The laws, projects, and systems he put into place helped China run smoothly. His changes helped China become one of the world's great nations.

▲ Qin Shi Huangdi used images of dragons, such as the one in this official seal, to show the strength of his empire. The seal was used to stamp documents.

Glossary

adviser person who gives help or advice

ancestor person from an earlier generation of a family

archaeologist person who finds out about the past by studying the remains of buildings and other objects

artifact object that was made or used by humans in the past

august grand and highly honored

crown prince person who will become the next ruler, usually ruler's oldest son

dagger short, pointed knife used as a weapon

dynasty powerful group or family that rules for a certain length of time

emperor ruler of an empire

empire large land or group of lands ruled by one person or government

festival special time of celebration

general leader in an army

harmony peaceful agreement

historian person who studies and writes about the past

hostage person held as a promise that an agreement will be kept

mercury metallic chemical element that is usually liquid and that can be poisonous

noble person of high birth or rank in society

pavilion open building used for entertainment or shelter

phosphorus white or yellow chemical element that is waxlike and sometimes has a faint glow

potion drink that is used as medicine or is supposed to have magical powers

ruin remains of something, such as a building, that was destroyed

scandal disgraceful or dishonorable action

scholar learned person

script characters used in written language

silk cloth woven from the fibers produced by silkworms

terra cotta brown-orange pottery made of baked or hardened clay

tomb burial place, often marked by a stone or building

tutor teacher hired to teach a child at home

Time Line

259 B.C.E.	Zheng is born in Qin
250 B.C.E.	Prince Zizhu comes to power as King Zhuang Xiang of Qin
247 B.C.E.	King Zhuang Xiang dies
246 B.C.E.	Zheng comes to power
221 B.C.E.	All Warring States are united under Qin's rule
	Zheng changes his name to Qin Shi Huangdi
213 B.C.E.	Qin Shi Huangdi orders the burning of the **empire's** books
212 B.C.E.	Qin Shi Huangdi buries 460 **scholars** alive at Xianyang
210 B.C.E.	Qin Shi Huangdi dies while traveling
	Hu Hai succeeds his father as **emperor**
207 B.C.E.	Hu Hai (now Er Shi) kills himself

Pronunciation Guide

Word	You say
Ankuo	AHN-kwo
feng shui	fung SHWAY
Hu Hai	hoo HIGH
Lao Zi	l'ow TSEE
Lu Buwei	LOO boo-WAY
Meng Tian	MUNG jhee-AN
Qin Shi Huangdi	chin SHER hwahng-DEE
Sima Qian	SEE-mah chee-AHN
Taoism	DOW-iz-um
Xianyang	shee-an-YAHNG
Xiao	SHEOW
Zhao Gao	jhow GOW
Zheng	JHUNG
Zhuang Xiang	JHWAHNG shee-AHNG
Zizhu	tsee-JHOO

More Books to Read

DuTemple, Lesley. *The Great Wall of China*. Minneapolis, Minn.: Lerner Publishing, 2002.

Harvey, Miles. *Look What Came from China*. Danbury, Conn.: Scholastic Library Publishing, 1999.

Rees, Rosemary. *The Ancient Chinese*. Chicago: Heinemann Library, 2002.

Shuter, Jane. *Ancient Chinese Art*. Chicago: Heinemann Library, 2002.

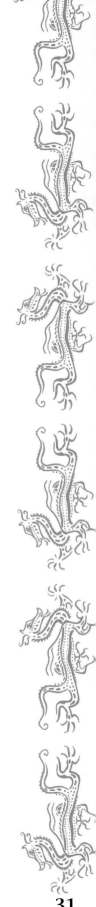

Index

Ankuo 10–11
archaeologists 5, 27
art and artists 5

book burnings 22, 23, 29
building projects 4, 20–21

children 9
China 4, 6, 13, 14, 18, 20, 29
clothing 9
Confucianism 16, 17

Duke Xiao 10–11

education 9
entertainment 9
Er Shi (Hu Hai) 26, 27, 28

feng shui 21
festivals 9
Fu Su 26, 27

Great Wall of China 4, 20–21, 23, 29

houses 9

jade 25
jewelry 9, 25
Jing Ke 13

Lao Zi 16, 17
laws 10, 17, 28, 29
Legalism 17
Li Si 12, 13, 17, 22, 26, 27, 28
Lu Buwei 11, 12

Meng Tian 20
money 18, 29
Mount Li 21, 28

nobles 8–9, 10

palaces 9, 12, 13, 14, 21, 24, 28

poison 13, 26
potions 24, 26

Qin 6, 7, 10, 12, 13, 14
Qin Shi Huangdi (Zheng) 4–5,
    12–13, 18–19, 20–21
    attempts to kill 13, 24
    becomes emperor 4, 14
    birth and early life 5, 6–7
    family 6, 7, 8, 10–11, 12–13
    fear of death 24–25, 26
    government and laws 12, 13,
    15, 17, 18–19, 22–23, 29
    illness and death 5, 26–27, 28
    tomb 4, 21, 27

religious beliefs 16–17
roads 18, 21

scholars 8, 19, 22–23
    killing of 23
Shang Yang 10
Shiji 4
Sima Qian 4
standardization 18–19

taiji (yin-yang) 17
Taoism 16, 17
terra cotta army 27
tiger tallies 15
trade 9

Warring States 6, 7, 13, 14, 15, 18
weights and measures 18, 29
writing 19, 29

Xianyang 14, 21, 26, 28

Zhao (state) 10, 11, 13
Zhao Gao 26, 27, 28
Zhao Ji 6, 11
Zhuang Xiang (Zizhu) 6, 7,
    10–11, 12